RHYTHMS OF THE HEART

A BOOK OF POEMS

By

DIVA JOAN CARTWRIGHT

RHYTHMS OF THE HEART

1st Edition

All poems and artwork in this book are by Joan Cartwright.

Published by Lulu.com

ISBN 978-1-4357-5614-4

To Eitra Snommis

TABLE OF CONTENTS

Dedication	iii
Change of Heart	2
Lover, infatuated with being loved	6
Him	8
Time Moves Too Slowly	10
The Man I Love	12
“How,” you ask, “do you know?”	13
In Love	14
A Love That’s True	15
Bright Moments	16
Bright Moments - Opus 2	17
FACT	18
A Special Prayer	19
Notes	20
List of Artwork	21

Other works by the author	21
About the author	22
Contact	24

THE POEMS

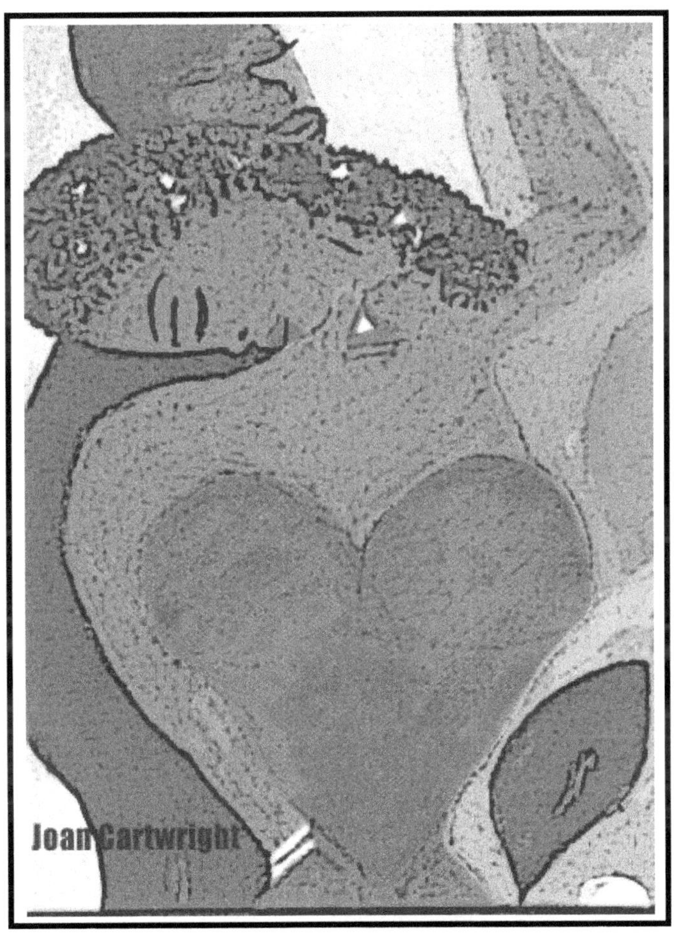

Change of Heart

While exploring for a poem of duress
He decided not to bother with bleak sadness
He set out to write a line
That would emulate the time
That he spent being foolish with his house guest

One very early summer morning she appeared
Looking strikingly alluring and demure
He kissed her perfumed gloves
Assured her of his love
Then careened and led her off into the house

Being tired from the ride, she fell to rest a bit
Her ruffled bodice opened to reveal her tit
He had contemplated reading while she slept

But, alas, he saw her loveliness
Was more in need of being with
His immediate reaction was to free her from the bind
That her riding clothes had pressed upon her form
At the very last waist button
His finger touched on something
That aroused his curiosity to venture on

There emerged a heart-shaped navel
Just as rounded as a grape
And as purple as a glass of wine could be
It was soft and slightly supple
Protruding like a nipple
And he wondered if he sucked it would she see

He ruffled her to check what state of sleep she'd found
Then, lowered to his knees, beside her on the ground
His tongue swept cross her navel

And left a gleam of spittle
Then, over come with lust, he bit and chewed the pimple

Awakened by the biting, she screamed and fought and scoffed
But by this time, his bulging pants
Had opened and were off
His rod, then, stood erect, electing her to gasp
And just as quick, she dropped her slip
While he undid her clasp

At once, they fell upon the bed
Writhing with the pain
That started at a navel, proving
Basic training's not in vain

Lover, infatuated with being loved

Overnight, I awaken

To desire's voice

Craving for more touches

I tingle inside

With the need

To have you, again

A reach ago

I searched for

What you have to give

While common sense crushed

My will to live

To have and be had

Even in rejection

There is the pleasure

Of knowing what not to want

Those silent screams echo

Pains of pure enjoyment

Love's Delight

Him

I like to be with him when I'm down

He lifts me up and spins me around

He turns up the corners of my pouting mouth

He makes me smile and all the while

I'm missing you

He only makes me miss you more

I kiss him and know it's you I'm for

It's you I desire

It's you I adore

But I get tired of crying

And my eyes get sore

So, I go to him when I'm missing you

I feel his hands

And think of love we knew

His gentle words make me feel sooo warm

As I welcome him into my arms

He suffocates my blues

And, for a while,

I stop missing you

Time Moves Too Slowly

Time moves too slowly

That's how I know

My heart cannot wait

To see your face

Since yesterday

It's been one thousand days

That we have touched

And loved so much

The minutes crawl by

As my heart dies

To cling to you

All night through

A year it's been

Since the moment when

I felt the grace

Of your embrace

The Man I Love

The man I love thinks

I'll see stars in his eyes

He'll be warm all the time

And I'll love him

“How,” you ask, “do you know?”

When you have looked forever

For a thing that seems a dream

And you think that never

Will you really see the gleam

Then you know you know

When truth has hit the light

And your missing hope

Has come into your sight

You know you know

That this time it is right

And it’s for you

You do

You know

In Love

I curl up on your chest where there is hair
And I'm aware you want me there

You kiss me on my lips
The taste is sweet
And I repeat
The kiss, complete

We hold each other tight
Within my arms
I feel your warm
Embracing charms

Our body language flows
As we make love
It's like a dove
In flight above

A Love That's True

If I never see another day

Because my life has flown away

It won't be bad for me, oh, no

Because I've know the love you show

If I chance to take but one more breath

And, then, go on to meet my death

I cannot be sad since I've found in you

A moment of a love that's true

Bright Moments

You brought the sun down from the sky
Put it in my heart and made me fly
You closed the book that spoke of pain
And, then, you talked to me about love and rain
We loved and laughed until we were spent
And now I'm filled with nothing but bright moments

Bright moments of love you gave to me
Bright moments of love for eternity
Bright moments of love you gave to me
Bright moments of joy for eternity

Bright Moments - Opus 2

Remember when we walked
Along the rushing city street
And you reached out to hold my face
To gently kiss my cheek?

Ah, bright moments
Sparkled in my heart
Every other moment
That we spent apart

FACT

There is nothing like a good fresh man!

DADDY'S SEED

A Special Prayer

Today, I said a special prayer to God
That you would always stay
I prayed that you would let me be
A bright moment for you each day

As you lay sleeping in my arms
It began to rain
I softly kissed your dreaming face
Then, fell asleep, again

NOTES

ARTWORK

1. LOVERS Cover
2. EITRA SNOMMIS iv
3. LOVERS (B&W) vl
4. THE MAN I LOVE THINKS 12
5. DADDY'S SEED 18
6. PHOTOGRAPH OF JOAN CARTWRIGHT AT AGE 32 20

OTHER WORKS BY THE AUTHOR

In Pursuit of a Melody (Trafford: 2006)

In Pursuit of a Melody CD (I AM Records: 2005)

Amazing Women in Jazz and Blues (Lecture)

Love Translation CD (I AM Records: 2008)

So, You Want To Be A Singer? A Manual for Up and Coming Divas (Lecture)

An Evening with Joan Cartwright and Jazz Hotline (I AM Records: 1995)

The Cultural Politics of Commercial Jazz (FAU Master's Thesis: 1994)

A History of African-American Jazz and Blues (FYICOMMINC: 1994)

ABOUT THE AUTHOR

Diva Joan Cartwright has toured five continents and 15 countries including the U.S.A., 8 European countries, Brazil, Mexico, Ghana, Gambia, South Africa, China and Japan, with her swinging brand of jazz and blues.

She is a composer and her book, **IN PURSUIT OF A MELODY** contains 40 original songs and lyrics to standard songs: ***A Night in Tunisia*** by Dizzy Gillespie, ***Blue Bossa*** by Kenny Dorham, ***Tune Up*** by Miles Davis and ***Bessie's Blues*** by John Coltrane. The companion CD contains 8 of Joan's original compositions.

Joan's book also contains two lectures that she's given to over 5,000 children and college students, in U.S., Switzerland, Sicily, China and Japan: ***WOMEN IN JAZZ*** and ***SO, YOU WANT TO BE A SINGER?*** Her workshops are dynamic and educational, highlighting the pitfalls and benefits of the music business. She contends that, Knowing music theory is a step in the right direction for any singer who truly wants to excel in the world of music!

Diva JC names any ensemble of musicians she works with ***Jazz Hotline***. Why? Because the music swings and it's always HOT! Her most famous Blues are *Nobody's Husband*, *Oh, Baby!* and *Treat Me Right*.

Known as the Hip Hop Mom of Atlanta, Joan performed Jazz Meets Hip Hop with her daughter's hip hop/soul group - Caustic Dames, in Florida, Georgia, Alabama, Italy, France and England. Hear Joan on Atlanta Has Spoken, a compilation of spoken word.

Joan Cartwright is available for bookings around the world. Her knowledge of music and her professional attitude enables Joan to travel alone and work with professional jazz and blues musicians, wherever she is contracted to perform.

During her 30-year career, Joan has performed with Lou Donaldson, Dr. Lonnie Smith, Freddie Hubbard, Dorothy Donegan, Philly Joe Jones, Shirley Scott and hundreds of musicians in the U.S., Europe and Asia!

This talented lady is bound to bring a smile to your face with her swinging jazz and blues! Don't miss the opportunity to enjoy her performance when she comes to your side of town!

IN PURSUIT
OF A MELODY
Joan Cartwright

Joan Cartwright
In Pursuit
Of A Melody

THE SIGN OF THE BLUES
by
Joan Cartwright, M.A.

So, You Want To Be A Singer?
by Joan Cartwright, M.A.

Contact:

Joan Cartwright
FYI Communications, Inc.
Women in Jazz South Florida, Inc.
2801 S. Oakland Forest Drive, Suite103
Oakland Park, FL 33309
954-607-7471 SKYPE
musicwoman08@yahoo.com

- www.divajc.com
- www.fyicomminc.com
- www.joancartwright.com
- www.wijsf.org
- www.blogtalkradio.com/musicwoman
- www.divajc.tv
- www.divajc.blip.tv
- www.mogulus.com/divajc
- www.myspace.com/divajoancartwright
- www.myspace.com/joancartwrightandjazzhotline
- www.myspace.com/jazzgiants
- www.myspace.com/jazzmeetshiphop
- www.myspace.com/musicwomanlive
- www.myspace.com/womeninjazz

www.wijsf.org

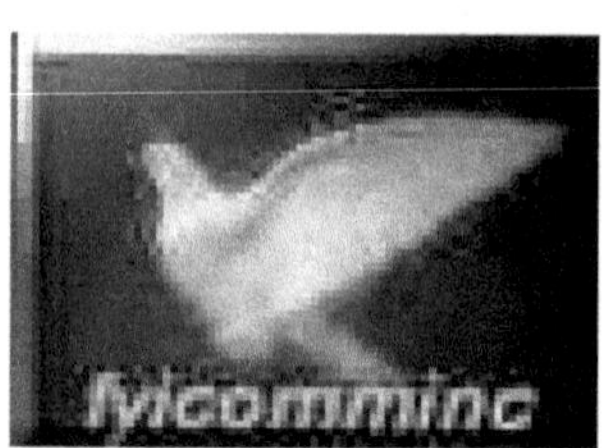

www.fyicomminc.com

www.ingramcontent.com/pod-product-compliance
Ingram Content Group UK Ltd.
Pitfield, Milton Keynes, MK11 3LW, UK
UKHW020227250726
13967UKWH00001B/234

9 781435 756144